T0054067

Who Were
The Wright Brothers?

Who Were
The Wright Brothers?

by James Buckley Jr.

illustrated by Tim Foley

Penguin Workshop

For the late Peter M. Wright, who, though not one of the
original Wright brothers, still gave me wings to write—JB

PENGUIN WORKSHOP
An Imprint of Penguin Random House LLC, New York

Text copyright © 2014 by James Buckley Jr. Illustrations copyright © 2014 by Tim Foley.
Cover illustration copyright © 2014 by Penguin Random House LLC. All rights reserved.
Published by Penguin Workshop, an imprint of Penguin Random House LLC, New York.
PENGUIN and PENGUIN WORKSHOP are trademarks of Penguin Books Ltd.
WHO HQ & Design is a registered trademark of Penguin Random House LLC.
Printed in the USA.

Visit us online at www.penguinrandomhouse.com.

Library of Congress Control Number: 2014939730

ISBN 9780448479514   20 19

Contents

Who Were
the Wright Brothers?

On May 25, 1910, Milton Wright took his first airplane flight. He had lived a long and busy life, working for his church, raising his family, and traveling. But he had never been in an airplane. Of course, in 1910, only a handful of people had!

Two people who did have flying experience were Milton's sons, Wilbur and Orville Wright, who had invented the airplane in 1903. Milton had watched them grow from curious and hard-working boys into two of the most famous men in the world.

The Wright brothers built and flew their plane only after years of trial, error, and hard work. From the early twentieth century to the present,

every single airplane ever built includes something
first created by the Wright brothers.

Their invention changed the world. However,

on this day in May of 1910, the brothers didn't care about the world. They were just happy to share their success and joy with their father, who had given them so much support.

On a field not far from their family home in Dayton, Ohio, Orville Wright settled his eighty-one-year-old father into the plane. Then Orville sat at the controls. The two men held on as the aircraft slowly got up to speed and then took off! They circled the field over and over, staying in the air for nearly seven minutes.

During the flight, Milton leaned toward his son. Over the roar of the engine, he shouted, "Higher, Orville . . . higher!"

So that's where Orville took Milton . . . and that's where the Wright brothers took the world.

Chapter 1
The Young Brothers

The Wright brothers, Reuchlin and Lorin, were born in Indiana. Reuchlin grew up to be a farmer, while Lorin worked as a bookkeeper.

Those Wright brothers had two younger brothers who grew up to become quite a bit more famous.

Wilbur Wright was born in Millville, Indiana in 1867, and Orville Wright was born four years later in Dayton, Ohio. Their younger sister, Katharine, was born in 1874. Their parents were Milton and Susan Wright.

Milton was a bishop in the Church of the United Brethren of Christ. He was also the editor of a United Brethren newspaper and a member of church councils. Milton traveled often to visit people in his church. As a bishop, he helped them organize their churches and listened to their problems.

While Milton traveled, Susan raised the five Wright children. Because the family moved several times when the children were young, Susan had to create a new homelife over and over. It helped that she was good at making and fixing things. She helped her children build a sled

and other toys. Wilbur and Orville always said
their love of mechanical things came from their
mother.

The Wright family lived in Indiana and Iowa,
but eventually settled in Dayton, Ohio in 1884. It
was a great place for boys to grow up, with many
friends nearby and places to explore.

Until his late teens, Wilbur spent most of his time with his older brothers, Lorin and Reuchlin. Wilbur was the youngest member of his brothers' singing club, the Dayton Boys. He played football for a school team, and some friends called him the fastest runner in town. He did well in school, getting good grades in math, Greek, Latin, science, and writing.

WILBUR WRIGHT

Young Orville had enormous curiosity and energy. He didn't want to do things like everyone else. His mother let him walk by himself to a nearby kindergarten when he was five. After about a month of school, Susan visited the teacher. She asked how Orville was doing. "Why, you know, since the first few days I haven't *seen* him. I supposed you had decided to keep him at home," the teacher said. It turned out Orville was spending his days at a friend's house instead of going to kindergarten!

Though Orville was

ORVILLE WRIGHT

bright, school was not his favorite place. In fact, one of his teachers put him in the front row just so she could keep an eye on him.

Away from school, Orville found ways to make money. He helped some of his friends put on a circus and arranged a parade through town to bring in customers for the show. With Wilbur, he built kites and other toys with which to play.

The brothers got plenty of support from their parents, who let them explore the world around them.

"We were lucky enough to grow up with encouragement to investigate whatever aroused our curiosity," Orville later wrote.

On returning from one of his trips, Milton gave Wilbur and Orville a small wooden toy. It looked a bit like a helicopter. The toy had a propeller and was powered by a rubber band. Invented by Frenchman Alphonse Pénaud, the toy would hover in the air for several seconds after the rubber band was wound up and released.

As the little toy zipped around their house, the Wright brothers were excited and amazed! Orville later said that they tried to make a larger version of it on their own, but "it failed to work so well." The toy fueled their imaginations and inspired their dreams of one day building a flying machine.

Chapter 2
Printers and Newsmen

In late 1885, when Wilbur was eighteen, he suffered an injury that changed his life. While

playing hockey on an icy pond with some friends, a hockey stick struck Wilbur in the face. Several of his teeth were knocked out, and he had other injuries. Though his face healed, other medical problems soon developed in his heart and stomach. He had wanted to become a teacher, but after the accident he left school to recover from his injuries. Wilbur became very depressed.

However, since he was at home, he was able to help his mother. By this time, Susan was very sick with tuberculosis, a deadly lung disease. Over the next few years, Wilbur spent much of his time helping his mother and comforting her.

"Such devotion of a son has rarely been equaled," wrote Milton.

When he wasn't helping Susan, Wilbur explored the family's huge library. He read books on history, science, nature, and religion. Wilbur's health problems kept him from graduating high school, but he never stopped learning.

Though the family worked hard to care for her, Susan became weaker. She died on July 4, 1889.

While Wilbur had been spending so much time helping and caring for their mother, Orville had been developing other interests. Even when he was still in high school, one of his many hobbies led to the first Wright brothers business.

Orville had been given woodcutting tools as a gift. Woodcuts are carvings on wooden blocks that are then covered with ink and pressed onto paper. The woodcuts got Orville interested in printing. His father approved. Milton always encouraged his sons to try new things. To help Orville, he gave him some work printing calling cards when Orville and his friend Ed Sines began a printing business. The friends later printed an issue of their school's magazine called *The Midget*.

Orville soon wanted to print more than just small cards and papers. But instead of buying a bigger press, he made his own. The printing press needed a large, flat surface as a base. Orville found a blank tombstone and he used that as the base! He then used scraps

of wood and springs from an
old carriage to finish the
press. His father and older
brothers bought him pieces
of type to use on the press.

With the new, larger
machine, Orville published his
own newspaper when he was just a teenager.
The first issue of the *West Side News* came out in
Dayton on March 1, 1889.

PRINTING PRESSES

IN THE WRIGHT BROTHERS' DAY, PRINTING WAS DONE USING SMALL PIECES OF TYPE SHAPED LIKE INDIVIDUAL LETTERS, PUNCTUATION MARKS, AND SPACES. THE LEAD SHAPES WERE LINED UP IN RACKS TO SPELL WORDS AND CREATE ARTICLES. THE PRINTER HAND-ROLLED INK ONTO THE LETTER RACKS, AND THE PRINTING PRESS THEN DID ITS JOB OF PRESSING PRINT ONTO PAPER AS IT ROLLED THROUGH THE MACHINE.

It included ads from local businesses and articles copied from bigger newspapers. Orville charged fifty cents for a year of the weekly paper. With his press, Orville also helped his friend Paul Dunbar create *The Tattler*, the newspaper for Dayton's African American community. By this time, black and white students attended the same schools in Ohio, unlike in many Southern states. This was not an issue for the Wrights. Inspired by their father's teaching, the Wright family believed in equal rights for all people.

Wilbur already had experience helping his father with the church newspaper. He decided to join his younger brother on the *West Side News,* and he became the paper's editor. He later joined the printing business, too. The newspaper would begin a partnership that lasted for the rest of their lives. Though each brother had his own personality and talents, they found that they fit together perfectly.

"From the time we were little children, my
brother Orville and myself lived together . . .
We talked over our thoughts and aspirations,"
Wilbur wrote many years later. "Nearly everything
that was done in our lives has been the result
of conversations, suggestions, and discussions
between us."

The weekly *West Side News* soon turned into a daily newspaper called the *Evening Item*. Although the *Item* lasted only a few months, Wright and Wright Printing was very successful. The brothers printed flyers, advertisements, stationery, and invitations for people in Dayton.

In 1892, Orville picked up a new hobby . . . and the Wright Brothers rode off in another direction.

Chapter 3
Wrights on Wheels

By the early 1880s, bicycles had been around for more than half a century, but most of them had been difficult to ride, expensive, and just plain dangerous. In England in 1885, John Starley invented the "safety cycle." It had solid wheels and a chain connecting the rear wheel to pedals. It started a bicycle craze that reached the United States in 1890 and increased US bicycle sales to 1.2 million in just five short years!

Bicycles became especially popular in small cities such as Dayton because bikes were much easier to care for than horses. Riders didn't need

to feed bikes and they could store them anywhere, not just in stables. No one in Dayton used cars yet, either. Though some early models had been made, cars would not be popular for decades.

In 1892, Orville and Wilbur each got a new bike and began to ride. Orville loved to ride fast. He entered and won a few local bicycle races. Wilbur, on the other hand, liked slower rides along country lanes.

Because their friends knew the brothers
were good at fixing things, they began bringing
bicycles into the print shop for the Wrights to
repair. Orville and Wilbur suddenly realized they
had a new business!

The Wright Cycle Exchange opened on Third
Street in Dayton in late 1892. The Wrights fixed
bicycles and sold parts and tires.

The brothers used their newspaper experience to help get new customers. They printed what looked like an issue of a newspaper and filled it with ads and information about their shop. They created a fake "exam" for local students in which all the answers were about their bicycles! The brothers also built a large bicycle for two riders, but to get people's attention, they made the wheels four feet tall!

In addition to selling several different brands of bikes, the Wrights decided to make their own. The Wrights made several types of bikes. The Van Cleve was the fanciest. It sold for $65, as much as a working man might earn in several months.

VAN CLEVE
BICYCLE

They also made a less expensive bike called the St. Clair. Today, only five bicycles made the by Wright Cycle Company still exist.

The brothers still lived at home with their father and Katharine. For fun, they would visit friends or have people come to their house to play music and sing together. Orville played the mandolin while Wilbur played harmonica.

However, the Wright brothers didn't pay much attention to dating. In fact, neither brother ever married.

However, their older brother Lorin's children often visited the family home, and Wilbur and Orville enjoyed playing with them. The children sometimes had to compete with the brothers to play with their own toys! Wilbur and Orville loved to tinker with anything they could get their hands on.

Chapter 4
Inspired to Fly

In early 1896, Orville became very ill with typhoid fever, a potentially deadly disease. Once again, Wilbur stepped in to care for a sick family member. Katharine was home from Oberlin

College in Ohio and she helped, too. Orville took six weeks to recover. Fortunately, business was slow at the bike shop in the winter, so Wilbur spent some time in the family library. He also kept up with the world news.

The last few decades of the 1800s were a golden age of invention. Thomas Edison invented the lightbulb and the record player. Alexander Graham Bell perfected the telephone. Several people were working on the first automobiles. Other inventors looked to

the sky. Around the world, men were trying to build flying machines and were experimenting with gliders. Newspapers carried stories of their attempts and their failures.

FLYING MACHINES

A GLIDER IS AN AIRCRAFT THAT STAYS ALOFT WITHOUT AN ENGINE. THE CRAFT FLOATS ON THE WIND AND CURRENTS OF AIR. A PAPER AIRPLANE IS A TYPE OF GLIDER. LARGER GLIDERS WERE THE FIRST TYPE OF WINGED AIRCRAFT TO CARRY A PILOT. PEOPLE HAVE BEEN EXPERIMENTING WITH GLIDERS FOR CENTURIES. THE FAMOUS ITALIAN SCIENTIST LEONARDO DA VINCI CREATED GLIDER DESIGNS IN THE 1400S AND 1500S.

OVER THE CENTURIES, INVENTORS TRIED MANY SHAPES OF GLIDERS—WIDE WINGS, FLAPPING WINGS, SHORT WINGS. THEY WERE TRYING TO IMITATE THE FLIGHT OF BIRDS. BY THE LATE 1800S, PEOPLE CHANGED GLIDERS TO AIRPLANES BY ADDING ENGINES. THE MORE POWER AN ENGINE HAD, THE MORE LIKELY THE AIRCRAFT COULD FLY. GLIDERS WERE THE FIRST STEPS TO MAKING HUMAN DREAMS OF FLIGHT COME TRUE.

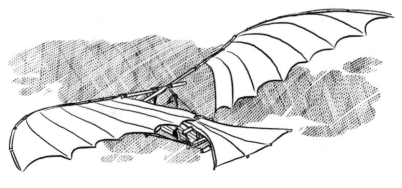

Samuel Langley was one of the early flying
pioneers. Langley was a famous scientist and head
of the Smithsonian Institution in Washington,
DC. In 1891, he built a steam-powered machine

he named the *Aerodrome*. Langley's first aircraft
did not have room for pilots, but some models
of the *Aerodrome* stayed in the air for several
minutes at a time.

Octave Chanute was also in the race to fly. A Frenchman who worked in America, Chanute was a successful railroad engineer. He used his knowledge to design wings that would help a glider stay in the air. One of his gliders was called the *Katydid*, after the leaflike insect. He tested them on sand dunes near Lake Michigan. In 1894, Chanute wrote a book about flying that Wilbur Wright read. Wilbur and Chanute would later exchange many letters about flying.

A German inventor, Otto Lilienthal, was perhaps the most successful aviator. He made more than two-thousand short flights in different gliders. He kept careful notes of how each glider performed. This information later helped the Wrights and other inventors construct their wings.

Sadly, Lilienthal died in August, 1896, when his glider crashed to the ground from more than fifty feet in the air.

The goal of all of these inventors was to create a flying machine that would carry a pilot. It would launch by itself, move through the air, and land safely. Wilbur read about all these inventors and began to consider joining them in the race to create such a machine.

Over the next few years, Wilbur studied aviation, even as the two brothers kept building bicycles. In 1899, he and Orville read a book about birds that gave them new ideas. "We could not understand that there was anything about a bird that would enable it to fly, that could not be built on a larger scale and used by man," Orville later said.

After several years of considering the idea, Wilbur wrote to the Smithsonian Institution in 1899. His letter said that he and his brother

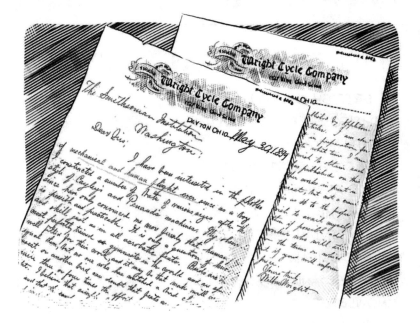

Orville had been "interested in human flight" since Milton had given the brothers the helicopter toy. In the letter, he asked for any papers the Smithsonian had on flying and a list of other places he could find information.

The Smithsonian office sent him a stack of papers and ideas on where he should look further. With this information in hand, the Wright Brothers got to work.

THE SMITHSONIAN INSTITUTION

BRITISH SCIENTIST JAMES SMITHSON LEFT HIS ENTIRE ESTATE "TO THE UNITED STATES OF AMERICA, TO FOUND AT WASHINGTON, UNDER THE NAME OF THE SMITHSONIAN INSTITUTION, AN ESTABLISHMENT FOR THE INCREASE AND DIFFUSION OF KNOWLEDGE AMONG MEN."

ALTHOUGH FOUNDED IN 1847 AS A CENTER FOR SCIENTIFIC RESEARCH, BEFORE LONG THE SMITHSONIAN ALSO BECAME THE HOME OF VARIOUS GOVERNMENT COLLECTIONS INCLUDING THOUSANDS OF PLANT AND ANIMAL SPECIMENS, ROCKS, SHELLS, MINERALS, AND EVEN JARS OF SEAWATER!

AMERICAN CITIZENS AND SCIENTISTS, SUCH AS WILBUR WRIGHT, LOOKED TO THE SMITHSONIAN AS A PLACE OF GREAT KNOWLEDGE AND LEARNING.

TODAY, THE SMITHSONIAN INSTITUTION IS THE CENTER OF NINETEEN MUSEUMS IN AND AROUND WASHINGTON, DC. IT IS THE WORLD'S LARGEST MUSEUM AND RESEARCH COMPLEX. CALLED "THE NATION'S ATTIC," IT HOLDS 137 MILLION DIFFERENT

ITEMS! THE WRIGHT BROTHERS' 1903 AIRPLANE HANGS ABOVE THE MAIN ROOM OF THE SMITHSONIAN AIR & SPACE MUSEUM.

Chapter 5
"That's Happiness!"

For the next year, Wilbur and Orville read and talked about flying. Their first step toward building a flying machine was to design and build a glider.

They first looked at the failed gliders of inventors who had tried before them. From their study, Wilbur and Orville decided that to build an aircraft, they had to solve three problems:

- building an engine that would make the aircraft move forward
- constructing a wing that would be able to lift the machine
- controlling the machine once it was in the air

The Wrights felt that the engine was the easiest problem to solve. They had already built a small engine for their shop, and other people had been successful building engines of various sizes. So they decided to tackle that problem last.

The Wrights looked at the wings Lilienthal and Chanute had designed already. They learned that a wing must be curved in a certain way so that as the air moves over the top of the wing, it creates lift. Lift is the upward force that opposes the pull of gravity to keep any flying machine in the air and off the ground. As with birds, the shape of the wing has to be just right. The Wrights tried many different designs and shapes of their own. They made their own tiny models of wings out of steel.

The problem of how to control the glider was the hardest to solve.

"The problem [of balance and control is] the problem of flight itself," Wilbur wrote.

As the Wrights studied and experimented, they searched for an answer. How can a pilot turn a plane and control it as it moves through the air? The brothers' experience on bicycles proved very useful. To turn a bike, the rider has to move the handlebars to one side. But the rider also has to lean into the turn and keep balanced while leaning. The Wrights felt that controlling a flying machine would be similar.

One day in the bicycle shop, Wilbur chanced on a key part of the solution. He was holding a long, thin cardboard box that had contained a bicycle tire's inner tube. As he held the box by the ends, he twisted it. Suddenly, he realized he had the answer! Twist the wings! If they could make

the wings of their glider twist slightly, or "warp," that might help the pilot control the turns.

The Wrights solved all the problems they faced as they designed their gliders with experimentation. It was not work to the brothers. It was fun. Wilbur's best skill was coming up with new ideas. Orville's skill with building things helped make those ideas real. Together, they made a perfect team.

Orville later remembered how they had felt during these early days of discovery. "Wilbur and I could hardly wait for morning to come, to get at something that interested us. That's happiness!"

As work on the glider progressed, the Wrights shared their ideas with their father. Though he was often away, traveling for his church, Milton continued to support his sons in their new efforts.

"We are soon leaving," Wilbur wrote to his father, "for experiments with a flying machine. It is my belief that flight is possible . . . I think there is a slight possibility of achieving fame and fortune from it."

Chapter 6
Off to Kitty Hawk

When their first glider was ready, the Wrights looked for a place to try it out. They needed steady wind to help the glider stay aloft. They wanted a place with sand or a beach so that they could have soft landings. They also wanted a place where few people could watch their experiments.

Wilbur wrote to the US Weather Service and asked where such a place might be found. From a list the service sent back, Wilbur picked Kitty Hawk, a town on one of the small islands that make up the Outer Banks of North Carolina.

Other than a trip to Chicago for the 1893

Columbian Exposition, the Wrights had not been outside of Ohio since they were boys. For Wilbur, then thirty-three years old, his first trip to Kitty Hawk in 1900 became quite an adventure.

Wilbur boxed up the parts of the glider and took a long train ride south. After the train trip to the coast, he had looked for a boat to take him out to the island. But the tiny town was so small, there was no regular ferry service. Wilbur convinced a fisherman to carry him and the boxes filled with glider parts across to Kitty Hawk. The boat turned out to be old, leaky, and slow! Wilbur

 had to help bail water out when a rainstorm hit. He thought the boat's galley, or kitchen, was dirty and disgusting. All he ate for the two-day journey was a jar of jelly Katharine had packed for him!

Wet and tired, Wilbur finally arrived on the
sand dunes of Kitty Hawk. He met the Kitty
Hawk postmaster, Bill Tate, one of the town's few
residents. He and Wilbur had exchanged letters
before the trip, so Tate knew about the brothers'
plans. Wilbur sank gratefully into a bed Tate
made up for him at his house.

Orville arrived several days later. He brought
food and other supplies for the brothers' camp.
Together, they set up a tent in which to live. Later,

they would build a shed to house the workshop for the gliders and airplanes and another to sleep in.

Kitty Hawk was a very different place than leafy, green Dayton. The wind blew almost all the time. The winter weather was chilly and often rainy. There were no shops for miles around, so the Wrights had to bring in or find all their food.

They were bothered by sand flies and other insects. "The mosquitoes chewed us clear through our underwear and socks . . . Misery! Misery!" wrote Orville.

Even with all the difficulties, Orville found things to like about this strange new place. In a letter to Katharine, he wrote, "This is a great country for fishing and hunting. The woods are filled with wild game. They say a few bears are prowling about!"

The Wrights stayed in Kitty Hawk for weeks at a time during each of the next three winters. They tested their gliders over and over. If something broke, they simply found a way to fix it by themselves.

Their gliders were made from wood and cloth. The parts were held together with wire and a few

metal hooks or brackets. There was no motor yet.
The brothers were still trying to solve the problem
of control. Most of these gliders had wings that
were about twenty to thirty feet across.

The brothers took turns lying facedown on the gliders. With help from Bill Tate and other local men, they pulled the gliders into the air by running down the slope of a sand dune. When the

runners let go, the pilot took over. Some flights lasted half a minute or so, but most lasted just a few seconds. With each flight or even with each hard landing, the Wrights learned something new. They were becoming experts in how things fly.

After their glider tests in 1901, Wilbur gave
a speech to a group of engineers in Chicago. He
described the things he and Orville had learned. It
was the first time that the Wright brothers' work
was made public. Orville relied on his brother to
be the "voice" of their mission, as he was terribly
afraid of public speaking.

In 1902, the Wrights returned to Kitty Hawk
with yet another glider design. They used the
lessons they had learned from earlier flights to
make this version even better. They had high

hopes, but the first several tests did not go well.
The glider often spun in a circle instead of flying
straight. One night, as Orville sat in his bunk,
listening to the howling winds outside, he had an
idea. What if the tail of the glider moved along
with the wings? That might prevent the spinning.
In the morning, he showed Wilbur his plan, and
they tried it. It worked! Once again, the brothers
had worked together, talking through ideas to
solve a problem.

The 1902 glider was soon soaring across the
dunes. On October 23, Orville set a new world
record for the longest glider flight. In twenty-six
seconds, he flew more than 622 feet.

They were sure they could now make a
powered airplane. Tired but excited, they headed
back to Dayton.

Chapter 7
The First Flights

The Wright brothers worked for the next year in Dayton on a bigger and better version of their glider design. They added a motor and propellers, transforming it into their first airplane. By December 1903, they felt they were ready to give it a test.

They were almost too late. On December 8, 1903, Samuel Langley launched the latest version of *Aerodrome*. This new model had a pilot. However, the *Aerodrome* plunged into the Potomac River, just south of Washington, DC, right after leaving the launching place. The pilot had to be rescued from the chilly water.

In a letter to Chanute, Wilbur wrote, "I see that Langley has had his fling . . . It seems to be

our turn to throw now . . . I wonder what our luck
will be?"

Once again, the Wrights headed to Kitty Hawk. They assembled their new machine in the shed they had built the year before. They called the airplane the *Wright Flyer*. Then they waited for the right weather. They needed wind, but not too much. They also didn't want to fly in the rain.

On December 14, the conditions were just right. To decide who would fly first, the brothers flipped a coin. Wilbur won. However, their first test of the *Wright Flyer* failed. Wilbur got only a few feet off the ground before the engine stalled. The machine crashed down to the ground, breaking several small parts.

By December 17, repairs were finished and conditions were perfect again. The brothers woke early and had a big breakfast. They hung a large flag on their sleeping hut. This was a signal to the men living down the beach at the US Lifesaving Station—an early version of the Coast Guard—

that the brothers needed help to move their heavy airplane into the correct position on the sand.

By 10:35 a.m., the men had arrived and the airplane was in position on the starting rail. This was a long, thin platform on which the airplane slid before starting—the first *Wright Flyer* did

not have wheels. One of the local men, John
T. Daniels, was told to snap a photo when the
plane took off. Daniels had never taken a picture
before! Wilbur set the camera up and told Daniel
to simply squeeze a small rubber ball to take the
picture.

The two brothers checked the airplane carefully. Then they shook hands. This was not something they normally did before flights. Daniels later said that the Wrights looked like men "who weren't sure they'd ever see each one another again."

Orville laid down on the pilot's controls. Wilbur stood at the end of the wing to steady the craft as the engine started. Slowly, the *Wright Flyer* moved down the rail. Wilbur ran alongside,

holding the wing. As the plane reached the end
of the rail, it rose into the air! Daniel snapped the
picture and captured the historic moment.

A human being was truly flying!

Orville's first flight lasted only twelve seconds
and he flew only 120 feet. But he had done it
with engine power, controlled steering, and a safe

landing. The Wright brothers had invented the airplane!

The men on the beach surrounded Orville, clapping and congratulating him. Wilbur shook his brother's hand again.

Over the next couple of hours, the Wrights made three more flights. Wilbur flew last and had the best flight of the day—which made it the best flight of all time to that point. He was in the air for fifty-nine seconds and flew 852 feet, more than two football fields.

As Wilbur climbed from the plane and the men congratulated him, a sudden wind gust lifted the plane! It tumbled down the beach. John T. Daniels tried to grab a wing, but he was pulled along in the wreckage. He was not hurt, but he would later boast of surviving the first airplane crash!

The *Wright Flyer* was badly damaged, however. It was in pieces all over the sand. The Wrights gathered up what they could and stored the wreckage in their work shed. Then they walked to town in Kitty Hawk to send a telegram back home to Dayton. The message read in part, "Success . . . four flights . . . longest 57 seconds . . . home Christmas."

The telegraph operator had made a mistake, changing fifty-nine seconds to fifty-seven seconds. Other mistakes about the flight soon followed. One newspaper in Virginia reported that the Wrights had soared for three miles over the ocean!

Incredibly, no major newspapers covered the story! Without seeing the airplane fly for themselves, many reporters thought the Wrights were making their story up.

In the Wright's home in Dayton, however, the telegram was received with joy. Milton Wright read it and then announced to his family, "The boys have flown."

Chapter 8
"Flyers or Liars?"

Returning to Dayton, Wilbur soon wondered, "What will we do with our baby?" The brothers knew they had made a successful airplane. They also knew they could do even better.

With their new airplane design, they no longer needed the high winds and soft sand of Kitty Hawk. Huffman Prairie, a field near Dayton, became their new testing ground. Over

the next two years, the Wrights made dozens of
test flights there. They made other versions of the
airplane, trying to make it fly faster and farther.
By 1905, the *Wright Flyer* was better than ever.
Orville once made a flight of nearly an hour,
circling high above the field. Neighbors came
out to watch "the boys" at their work. A streetcar
line ran right by the field, so travelers sometimes
watched in amazement as the brothers soared.
Milton came out to watch as well, proud of what
his sons had accomplished.

Even though many local people saw the Wrights fly, few outside Dayton realized what the brothers had achieved. For those who had not witnessed the brothers' flights, there was no proof to verify the story because they hadn't allowed photographers at their test flights. Very few reporters bothered to travel to Ohio to witness the test flights, so newspapers did not cover the story.

The Wright brothers kept working. Once they had perfected their 1905 airplane, they wanted to find a way to sell it. They had gotten into flying simply to experiment and learn. Once they were successful, they knew they could make money, too.

Orville and Wilbur became very worried about someone stealing their idea. To prevent that, after they finished work on the 1905 airplane, the Wright brothers didn't fly for almost three years. In the meantime, they worked hard to sell their ideas to the US Army. The Wrights thought that the military could use their new invention. To the brothers' shock, the army said no. Many people had written to the army and the government claiming to have invented flying machines. The army thought the Wrights were more of the same—crackpots with wild dreams but no real success.

In spring of 1908, the Wrights went back to Kitty Hawk to test new improvements to their airplane. A few reporters were still chasing the rumors about the flying brothers. The reporters

went to Kitty Hawk, too, but didn't tell the Wrights. They hid in trees near the beach and watched with binoculars as Orville and Wilbur flew their airplane again and again. For the first time, newspapers in New York City and Paris published stories about the Wrights' success in

the air. (Orville later said that the brothers knew the men were watching!)

In France, where many aviation pioneers lived, not everyone believed the stories. A French newspaper wondered whether the Wrights were "flyers or liars?"

To put all doubts to rest, the Wrights arranged two important exhibitions of their work. Wilbur went to France to fly in Paris. Orville finally got the US Army to agree to take a look at the airplane. He went to Fort Myer in Virginia to demonstrate its success.

Chapter 9
Worldwide Fame

In Paris, Wilbur worked for several weeks putting his airplane together. Dozens of aviation experts came to the workshop, asking question after question. Thanks to a pilot named Alberto Santos-Dumont and other inventors, the French aviators believed *they* were the world trailblazers for flight. They did not want an American to swoop in and steal their glory.

On August 8, 1908, hundreds of people turned out to watch Wilbur's demonstration. The field was the center of a large horseracing track in Le Mans, a town near Paris.

Wilbur set the airplane on the launching rail. A movie filmed that day shows him carefully checking over the plane and the engine. Finally,

he was ready. He took his seat and adjusted the controls.

"Gentlemen," he said over the roar of the engines. "I am going to fly."

As the amazed spectators watched, Wilbur
roared into the sky and circled the field. He did
figure-eights, he flew high, and then he flew low,
not far over their heads.

The French admitted defeat. "We are beaten," one newspaper wrote, "It was not merely a success but a triumph . . . [It] will revolutionize . . . the world."

The reports from France finally convinced the world. Though the brothers had been able to fly for five years, very few had heard of their success. Even fewer had believed it. The flights in Paris were the clincher. The Wrights' airplane flew . . . and now everybody knew it.

Wilbur flew at the field for several more days. The crowds of people grew with each flight. Thousands came out to see this amazing invention. Wilbur was an overnight star in France. His picture appeared on magazines and newspapers. He was treated to dinners and special events. The hat he wore while flying was copied and sold in Paris shops. It was called the "Veelbur Reet," which is how French people were pronouncing his name.

FRANCE'S FIRST

THOUGH HE WAS BORN IN BRAZIL, ALBERTO SANTOS-DUMONT SPENT MOST OF HIS LIFE IN FRANCE. HE ALSO SPENT HUNDREDS OF HOURS IN THE AIR. SANTOS-DUMONT HAD A LARGE FAMILY FORTUNE FROM COFFEE FARMS IN BRAZIL. HE USED SOME OF HIS MONEY TO BUILD HUGE HOT-AIR BALLOONS, COMPLETE WITH A HANGING BASKET FOR THE PILOT. HE WON SEVERAL FRENCH PRIZES FOR FLYING HIS BALLOON FASTER AND FARTHER THAN MANY OTHERS. SANTOS-DUMONT BECAME WORLD FAMOUS AS ONE OF THE GREATEST BALLOON PILOTS.

BUT HE WANTED TO DO MORE. HE WORKED FOR SEVERAL YEARS ON AN AIRPLANE DESIGN, AND IN 1906—AFTER SEVERAL FAILURES—HE SUCCEEDED. SORT OF. A PLANE HE CALLED 14-BIS FLEW FOR

ABOUT SIX-HUNDRED FEET. HOWEVER, IT FLEW ONLY IN A STRAIGHT LINE AND COULD NOT TURN. IT ALSO FLEW THREE YEARS *AFTER* THE WRIGHT BROTHERS' FIRST FLIGHTS IN 1903. BECAUSE AT THAT TIME FEW PEOPLE BELIEVED IN THE WRIGHT BROTHERS' ACCOMPLISHMENTS, MOST EUROPEANS CALLED SANTOS-DUMONT THE "FIRST TO FLY." WILBUR WRIGHT SHOWED THEM OTHERWISE WITH HIS 1908 PARIS DEMONSTRATIONS.

Wilbur put up with all the attention. He did not like it very much, but he knew that fame would help him and Orville sell their invention.

About a month later, in Virginia, Orville repeated Wilbur's success. Government officials, army officers, and civilians looked to the sky for the first time. Orville soared above cheering and shouting crowds.

Teddy Roosevelt Jr., the son of the president, was at the field. Later he said, "I'll never forget their gasps of astonishment . . . it was a sound of complete surprise."

The US Army finally gave the brothers a contract to produce planes for the United States and to train new pilots.

Wilbur remained in France until the end of the year. During his exhibitions, he carried more than fifty people on their first airplane flights. One was an eleven-year-old boy! To show what the *Wright Flyer* could do, he also entered competitions and captured several flying prizes for distance and height. The biggest prize was twenty-thousand francs (about $4,000) for making the longest flight of 1908, a flight of more than two hours that he made on December 28.

By early 1909, Orville and Katharine joined Wilbur in Europe. Together again, the family

continued a triumphant tour. The brothers flew
in front of kings: Edward VII of England, Italy's
Victor Emmanuel, and Alfonso XIII of Spain.
During a flight in Italy, Wilbur took a cameraman
aloft. The film he shot was the first ever made
from an airplane. During this time, Katharine
also took her first flights with the brothers.

Though they were now world famous, the
Wrights didn't change. They were still calm,

quiet, and thoughtful men from Ohio. The rest
of their family watched proudly from America.
Milton wrote to his sons, "Be men of the highest
type." Wilbur answered, "I am sure Orville and
myself will do nothing which will disgrace the
training we received from you and Mother."

After returning from Europe, the brothers
earned more acclaim in the United States. They
received gold medals from Congress and the
Smithsonian Institution, along with awards

from flying clubs. President William Howard Taft invited them to the White House and congratulated them on their success.

After their long journey, the Wright brothers went home. The City of Dayton put on the Wright Brothers Home Days Celebration. Bands played, fireworks boomed, and speeches were made. A huge group of schoolchildren formed a "living flag." It was a joyous homecoming.

Chapter 10
Legacy in the Air

After the celebration in Dayton, the brothers got back to work. They had to make airplanes for the army, and they wanted to show their skills to their countrymen. Orville stayed home to start building their new airplane company, while Wilbur added another amazing flight to his career.

In October 1909, New York City was holding a large celebration in honor of explorer Henry Hudson, the Dutchman who had first sailed up the Hudson River three- hundred years

earlier. During the celebration, hundreds of ships filled the city's harbor. More than a million people filled the streets of Manhattan, and Wilbur gave them quite a show. He flew a *Wright Flyer* around New York Harbor and circled the Statue of Liberty. Then he flew up the Hudson River as people watched from the docks and rooftops of the city.

Not long after Wilbur returned from New York, the Wright Airplane Company opened in Dayton. It had a large factory and a warehouse. Dozens of men were hired to make Wright planes for sale to the US Army and to companies in Europe. The

Wrights also began training new pilots. Wilbur and Orville were the first people to fly, but they knew that others needed to learn so their new business could succeed. In 1911, one of the pilots they trained was Calbraith Rodgers.

The Wrights' success inspired others to jump into the airplane business. Some companies tried to use the Orville and Wilbur's ideas and designs without permission. For several years, the brothers fought to protect their inventions. Wilbur was so

busy suing copycat inventors that he had no time to fly.

He traveled back to France, Germany, and England to defend their invention in European courts. He made his last flight in May 1910 around the same time that Orville took their father aloft for the first time.

Wilbur had been working and traveling nonstop for years. During a trip to Boston in spring, 1912, he became very ill with a serious infection called typhoid. Though doctors did all that they could, Wilbur died on May 30 in Dayton with his family by his side. He was only forty-five years old.

He lived, as his father wrote, "a short life, full of consequences."

After Wilbur died, Orville lost interest in running the Wright Company. It was just not the same without his brother at his side. In 1915, Orville sold his part of the Wright Company for $1 million and retired.

CALBRAITH RODGERS AND THE VIN FIZ

PILOTING A WRIGHT AIRPLANE, CALBRAITH RODGERS WAS THE FIRST PERSON TO FLY ACROSS THE ENTIRE COUNTRY. THE AIRPLANE WAS CALLED THE *VIN FIZ*, AFTER A SODA COMPANY THAT SPONSORED THE FLIGHT. THE CROSS-COUNTRY TRIP WAS NOT EXACTLY NONSTOP. RODGERS TOOK OFF FROM NEW YORK ON SEPTEMBER 17, 1911. HE COULD ONLY FLY DURING THE DAY, SINCE THERE WERE NO LIT FIELDS. A SPECIAL TRAIN FOLLOWED HIS ROUTE TO PROVIDE HIM WITH FUEL AND A PLACE TO SLEEP EACH NIGHT. THE NOVELTY OF THE FLIGHT DREW CROWDS AND ADVERTISED VIN FIZ GRAPE SODA WHEREVER HE WENT.

DURING THE FLIGHT, NOT EVERYTHING WENT SMOOTHLY. RODGERS CRASHED THE PLANE MORE THAN A DOZEN TIMES! HE SUFFERED SEVERAL INJURIES AND ONCE HAD TO SPEND TWO DAYS IN A HOSPITAL. HE HAD TO ATTACH CRUTCHES TO THE PLANE BECAUSE HE NEEDED THEM TO WALK AFTER HE LANDED! THROUGH IT ALL, HE PERSEVERED. HE FINALLY REACHED LONG BEACH, CALIFORNIA, ON DECEMBER 10. HE HAD FLOWN MORE THAN FOUR THOUSAND MILES IN A TOTAL OF EIGHTY-TWO HOURS OVER EIGHTY-FOUR DAYS, BECOMING THE FIRST PERSON TO FLY ACROSS THE UNITED STATES.

In Dayton, Orville lived in Hawthorn Hill, the huge mansion the brothers had designed. It became home to Orville, Milton, and Katharine Wright for most of the rest of their lives. In 1926, Katharine married Harry Haskell, a man she first had met at Oberlin College, where she had studied to be a teacher. Sadly, Katharine died of pneumonia only three years later.

Orville continued to promote Wright Flyers and the idea of air travel. In 1932, he helped unveil a marker in Kitty Hawk at the new Wright Brothers National Monument. It was the largest US monument ever built to honor a living person. Back home, he never stopped making things. He often worked on the plumbing and heating systems at Hawthorn Hill. He created toys such as a dancing wooden clown for his nieces and nephews.

In the years after Wilbur's death, Orville watched their invention change the world. Airplanes got bigger and faster. People flew over the oceans and around the world. During World War II, Orville saw the power of his airplanes in war. He lived long enough to see the creation of jet airplanes and to read about an airplane breaking the sound barrier. In 1948, at age seventy-six, Orville Wright died after two heart attacks.

In 1969, US astronauts Neil Armstrong and Buzz Aldrin were the first men to reach the moon. To honor the pioneers of flight, they

carried small pieces of the first Wright brothers' airplanes with them in the space capsule.

Today, it's hard to imagine a world without airplanes. Through their brilliant ideas, hard work, and determination, the Wright brothers gave the world its future in the air.

TIMELINE OF
THE WRIGHT BROTHERS' LIVES

1867 ——Wilbur Wright is born in Indiana

1871 ——Orville Wright is born in Ohio

1889 ——The brothers publish a newspaper, the *West Side News*, in Dayton

1892 ——They start the Wright Cycle Exchange to repair and sell bicycles

1899 ——Work begins in earnest on the Wrights' early glider designs

1900 ——The Wrights make the first of their trips to Kitty Hawk, North Carolina, to test glider designs

1902 ——The Wrights fly their most successful glider

1903 ——The Wright brothers' airplane becomes the first in history to fly

1905 ——Working near their home in Dayton, the Wrights refine their airplane design

1908 ——Successful demonstrations in Paris and Virginia finally convince the world of the Wright brothers' success

1909 ——The Wrights form a company to make airplanes

1912 ——Wilbur Wright dies at age forty-five

1915 ——Orville Wright sells his share of the Wright airplane company

1929 ——Katharine Wright dies at age fifty-four

1932 ——A monument to the Wright brothers is completed and dedicated at Kitty Hawk

1948 ——Orville Wright dies at age seventy-six

TIMELINE OF
THE WORLD

Yellowstone becomes the first National Park ——— 1872

The Statue of Liberty is completed and dedicated ——— 1886
in New York Harbor

Great Columbian Exposition and World's Fair ——— 1893
is held in Chicago

The first modern Olympic Games are held ——— 1896
in Athens, Greece

The Model T, one of the first cars made for wide sale, ——— 1908
debuts from the Ford Company

The *Titanic* sinks on its first trip from England ——— 1912
to America

World War I begins in Europe ——— 1914

The Russian Revolution removes the czar from power ——— 1917
and sets up a new communist government

The Jazz Singer, the first movie with synchronized sound, ——— 1927
premieres

After a stock-market crash, America enters ——— 1929
the Great Depression

World War II begins in Europe ——— 1939

Two atomic bombs are dropped from airplanes ——— 1945
by the United States onto cities in Japan,
leading to the end of World War II

The United States spacecraft *Apollo XI* lands on the Moon. ——— 1969
Neil Armstrong and Buzz Aldrin become the first humans
to walk on the Moon

Columbia is the first space shuttle to take off and land ——— 1981
after visiting space

BIBLIOGRAPHY

Crouch, Tom. **The Bishop's Boys: A Life of Wilbur and Orville Wright**. New York: Norton, 1991.

Dixon-Engel, Tara, and Mike Jackson. **The Wright Brothers: First in Flight**. New York: Sterling, 2007

Freedman, Russell. **The Wright Brothers: How They Invented the Airplane**. New York: Holiday House, 1991

Kelley, Fred. **The Wright Brothers: A Biography Authorized by Orville Wright**. New York: Harcourt Brace, 1943.

Wescott, Lynanne and Paula Degen. **Wind and Sand: The Story of the Wright Brothers at Kitty Hawk**. New York: Harry Abrams, 1983

Kitty Hawk: The Wright Brothers' Journey of Invention. DVD. Directed by David Garrigus, 2003.

The Wright Stuff: The Life of Orville and Wilbur Wright. DVD. American Experience. Directed by Nancy Porter, 2003.

WEBSITES

Air and Space Museum
airandspace.si.edu/wrightbrothers/index_full.cfm
The Smithsonian Institution helped Wilbur Wright learn more about flying. The Smithsonian now has a large website to help you learn more about the Wright brothers. See photos of their aircraft, their personal belongings, and even Wilbur's report card!

Wright Brothers Memorial
nps.gov/wrbr/index.htm
Near the site of the Wright brothers' first flight, the National Park Service runs the Wright Brothers Memorial. This website includes information about the park, as well as information about the Wrights and their aircraft.

Wright Brothers Online Museum
wright-brothers.org
The Wright Brothers Aeroplane Company (using the old spelling for "airplane") is the name of a jam-packed online museum about the brothers and their lives. Its resources section also leads you to many other places to learn about the Wrights.

Wright Brothers' Flying Machine
pbs.org/wgbh/nova/wright
Many movies have been made about the Wright brothers, helped by their early use of photography and even film to document their work. This PBS site includes information from one of the documentaries. An interactive game lets you pilot the original *Wright Flyer*.